ILLUSTRATED BY

BRYAN COLLIER

RAÚL COLÓN

DIANE GOODE

MARY GRANDPRÉ

JOHN HENDRIX

YUYI MORALES

JON J MUTH

LEUYEN PHAM

SONIA LYNN SADLER

CHRIS SOENTPIET

KATHARINE LEE BATES

America the Beautiful
TOGETHER WE STAND

ORCHARD BOOKS • NEW YORK • AN IMPRINT OF SCHOLASTIC INC.

O beautiful for spa

"We become not a melting

pot but a beautiful

mosaic. Different people,

different beliefs, different

yearnings, different

hopes, different dreams."

JIMMY CARTER

cious skies,

Illustrations by Chris Soentpiet

"I believe . . .

that every human mind

feels pleasure in doing

good to another."

Thomas Jefferson

Illustrations by Mary GrandPré

For amber

waves of grain,

For purple mounta

in majesties

"Four score and seven years ago our fathers brought forth on this continent, a new nation, conceived in liberty, and dedicated to the proposition that all men are created equal."

ABRAHAM LINCOLN

Illustrations by Sonia Lynn Sadler

Above

the fruited plain!

America!

"Change will not come if we wait for some other person or if we wait for some other time. We are the ones we've been waiting for. We are the change that we seek."

BARACK OBAMA

Illustrations by Bryan Collier

"And so, my fellow

Americans: ask not what

your country can do for

you—ask what you can

do for your country."

JOHN F. KENNEDY

Illustrations by Jon J Muth

America!

God shed His grac

e on thee

"The test of our progress

is not whether we add

more to the abundance

of those who have much;

it is whether we provide

enough for those who

have too little."

FRANKLIN D. ROOSEVELT

Illustrations by Yuyi Morales

"It's wonderful what

we can do if we're

always doing."

GEORGE WASHINGTON

Illustrations by Diane Goode

And crown

thy good

with

brotherhood

"*Keep your eyes on the stars, but remember to keep your feet on the ground.*"

THEODORE ROOSEVELT

Illustrations by LeUyen Pham

"This is America . . .

a brilliant diversity

spread like stars, like

a thousand points of

light in a broad and

peaceful sky."

GEORGE H.W. BUSH

Illustrations by John Hendrix

From sea to

shining sea!

STATUE OF LIBERTY

The Statue of Liberty stands as a symbol of hope and freedom for people from all over the world. Given to the United States as a gift by the people of France, it was dedicated in October 1886.

CONSTITUTION

The Constitution established the rules and framework of our government. This included the creation of three separate and equal branches of government: the legislative, executive, and judicial branches.

AMERICAN FLAG

The American flag is one of the most important symbols of our country. It celebrates the United States' fifty states with fifty stars and remembers our thirteen original colonies with thirteen red and white stripes.

LIBERTY BELL

The Liberty Bell has long been associated with the idea of liberty and the fight for freedom. The Liberty Bell was among the bells rung at the first reading of the Declaration of Independence in 1776.

WHITE HOUSE

The White House in Washington, D.C., is the official residence of the President of the United States and his family. Theodore Roosevelt gave the White House its official name in 1901.

AMERICAN BALD EAGLE

As the United States' national bird, the powerful and majestic bald eagle is a symbol of freedom and liberty. The bald eagle is found in nature only in North America; it is depicted on the Great Seal of the United States.

AMERICAN ROSE FLOWER

The rose has a rich history in the United States, from the roses bred by George Washington to the White House's present-day Rose Garden. It was chosen as our national flower by Ronald Reagan in 1986.

WASHINGTON MONUMENT

The Washington Monument was built in honor of our first president, George Washington. This monument is located in the National Mall in Washington, D.C., and is the world's tallest stone structure.

MOUNT RUSHMORE

The faces of George Washington, Thomas Jefferson, Theodore Roosevelt, and Abraham Lincoln are carved into the side of Mount Rushmore, located near Keystone, South Dakota.

CAPITOL BUILDING

The Capitol Building in Washington, D.C., is a symbol of our country's representative democracy. Here, the United States Congress, made up of the House of Representatives and the Senate, works on making laws.

America the Beautiful

O beautiful for spacious skies,

For amber waves of grain,

For purple mountain majesties

Above the fruited plain!

America!

America!

God shed His grace on thee

And crown thy good

with brotherhood

From sea to shining sea!

O beautiful for pilgrim feet,
Whose stern impassioned stress
A thoroughfare for freedom beat
Across the wilderness!
America! America!
God mend thine every flaw,
Confirm thy soul in self-control,
Thy liberty in law!

O beautiful for heroes proved
In liberating strife,
Who more than self their country loved,
And mercy more than life!
America! America!
May God thy gold refine
Till all success be nobleness
And every gain divine!

O beautiful for patriot dream
That sees beyond the years
Thine alabaster cities gleam,
Undimmed by human tears!
America! America!
God shed His grace on thee
And crown thy good with brotherhood
From sea to shining sea!

OUR DEMOCRACY

America's government is based on a democratic system. It is one of our most valuable and cherished gifts from our founding fathers.

The word "democracy" comes from two Greek words: "Demos," which means PEOPLE, and "Kratos," which means POWER. In a democracy, the people elect a government to represent them. The government is responsible for maintaining the freedom and well-being of all citizens. President Lincoln defined our democracy as a government "of the people, by the people, for the people." In order to have freedom, we need laws that are enforced to guarantee our freedom. In America, everyone has an opportunity to be heard by voting.

Protecting our democracy is hard work and requires the active participation of us all.

★ ★ ★ ★ ★ ★ ★ ★ ★ ★ ★ ★ ★ ★ ★ ★ ★ ★ ★

"We hold these truths to be self-evident: that all men are created equal; that they are endowed by their Creator with certain unalienable rights; that among these are life, liberty, and the pursuit of happiness."

THOMAS JEFFERSON
from the Declaration of Independence

★ ★ ★ ★ ★ ★ ★ ★ ★ ★ ★ ★ ★ ★ ★ ★ ★ ★ ★

KATHARINE LEE BATES

Born in Massachusetts in 1859, Katharine Lee Bates was a poet as well as an English professor at Wellesley College.

Her poem "America the Beautiful" was inspired by the sights she saw during a trip from Massachusetts to Colorado in 1893.

"America the Beautiful" soon became one of our most beloved patriotic songs. Its heartwarming lyrics have filled Americans with pride for more than a century. Some of the song's admirers have proposed that it replace "The Star-Spangled Banner" as the national anthem.

Text copyright © 1910 by Katharine Lee Bates • All rights reserved. Published by Orchard Books, an imprint of Scholastic Inc., *Publishers since 1920.* ORCHARD BOOKS and design are registered trademarks of Watts Publishing Group, Ltd., used under license. SCHOLASTIC and associated logos are trademarks and/or registered trademarks of Scholastic Inc. No part of this publication may be reproduced, stored in a retrieval system, or transmitted in any form or by any means, electronic, mechanical, photocopying, recording, or otherwise, without written permission of the publisher. For information regarding permission, write to Orchard Books, Scholastic Inc., Permissions Department, 557 Broadway, New York, NY 10012.

Library of Congress Cataloging-in-Publication Data Available

ISBN 978-0-545-49207-2 • 10 9 8 7 6 5 4 3 2 1   13 14 15 16 17

Printed in the U.S.A.   113 • First printing, January 2013

Illustrations on pages 6–7 © 2013 by Chris Soentpiet • Illustrations on pages 8–9 © 2013 by Mary GrandPré • Illustrations on pages 10–11 © 2013 by Raúl Colón • Illustrations on pages 12–13 © 2013 by Sonia Lynn Sadler • Illustrations on pages 14–15 © 2013 by Bryan Collier • Illustrations on pages 16–17 © 2013 by Jon J Muth • Illustrations on pages 18–19 © 2013 by Yuyi Morales • Illustrations on pages 20–21 © 2013 by Diane Goode • Illustrations on pages 22–23 © 2013 by LeUyen Pham • Illustrations on pages 24–25 © 2013 by John Hendrix

The text was set in Bookman Old Style. • Book design by David Saylor and Charles Kreloff

We gratefully acknowledge Dr. William Bushong, Historian, White House Historical Association, for his invaluable consultation on the finished proofs; and Ronald B. Roth, Executive Editor, Grolier Multimedia Encyclopedia, and Scott Monje, Senior Editor, Encyclopedia Americana, for their astute, generous, and meticulous fact-checking of the text.

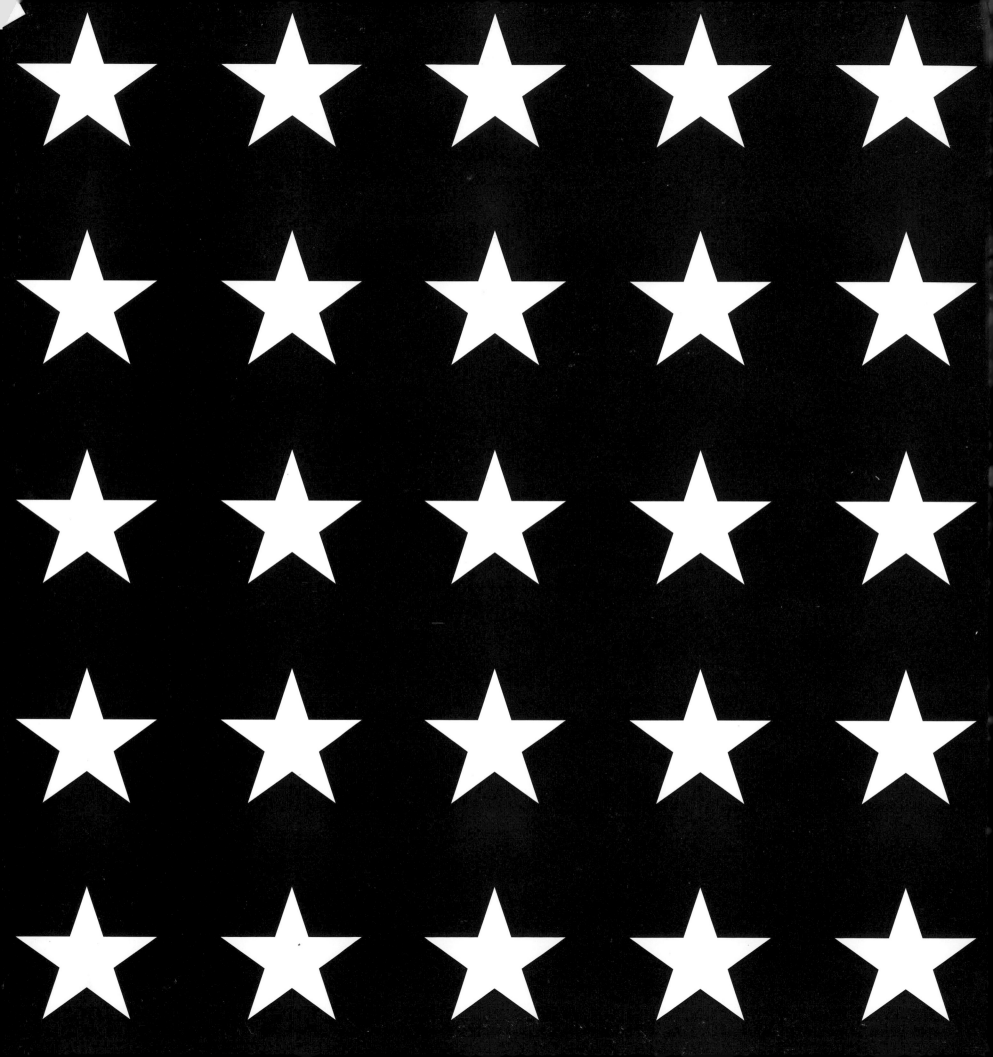